Online meetings
A facilitator's guide

Phil Green & Clive Shepherd

onlignment

ISBN: 978-1-4466-2795-2

First published in 2011

http://www.onlignment.com/

Online meetings
A facilitator's guide

onlignment

Preface

We can't go on meeting like this

Business Continuity Management is about how to stay in business when disaster strikes. Most organisations do it by choice; some are compelled to do it by law.

Since the beginning of 2009, Europe has endured a severe winter, a flu pandemic, the threat of industrial action and the vomiting of fine ash from the Eyjafjallajokull volcano.

It makes a massive impact upon an organisation's prosperity when people can no longer come together to communicate as normal.

Wherever you choose to look, the evidence shows that meetings are a fact of life, no matter if yours is a one-person business or a public company. You must connect with customers, suppliers, colleagues and managers.

In the USA it would be common for a person in business to take part in 3 meetings every day and make 4 or 5 business trips by plane each month. Cost is a good indicator too. Speaking in 2008, a prominent strategic meetings management firm calculated the annual spend on meetings to be €350 billion globally.

So where does this lead us?

1. Organisations are not going to stop holding meetings.

2. The risk of disruption to travel is ever-present.

3. Every organisation has to have a contingency plan to allow meetings to happen when it is not possible to bring people together face-to-face. They need a Plan B.

4. For most organisations, online meetings are the only feasible Plan B, both practically and economically.

5. Online meetings are only going to do the job if they are properly planned and facilitated.

In the rest of this e-book, we'll be outlining the **ten factors** that we believe make the difference between mere survival and gaining a competitive edge. We hope to prove that you can both reduce the cost of your meetings and at the same time raise their effectiveness. If that becomes reality, you might be tempted to let your Plan B become your Plan A!

And the ten factors are ...

1

Rehearse your business case

At the present time, with so much potential for disruption to travel plans, making a business case for online meetings is rather like arguing the ROI of emergency evacuation procedures. Who knows where and when fire will break out; no-one expects it. However, Business Continuity Management is not the only argument.

Online meetings cost less

Meetings are expensive. Gartner suggests they might represent one of the largest costs to enterprise, second only to labour.

Online meetings cost less. IBM estimates that an in-person meeting costs about US$600 per hour whereas a web conference is about US$6 per hour. This insight helps them to save over US$4 million in travel expenses per month using instant messaging and web conferencing.

> IBM estimates that an in-person meeting costs about US$600 per hour, whereas a web conference costs US$6.

So even if some emergency has not prevented a face-to-face meeting, there are valuable benefits from meeting online. Firstly, you don't need to book and set up a venue, and so you save the cost of:

- a venue (even in-house meeting rooms cost money to provide);

- power (lighting, heating, powering equipment);

- equipment (video camera, sound-recorder, TV, video player, projector);

- consumables (whiteboard, markers, stationery);

- meals and refreshments.

Secondly, you do not have to bring remote people to a venue, so you save the cost of travel and board and lodging.

You also recover opportunity costs such as loss of productivity due to absence and time spent in travelling. A person can take part in a single day in meetings that might have needed to be in different locations.

Online meetings also tend to be shorter and more focused since they do not include the same degree of socialising.

Of course online meetings are not cost-free, but many of the costs, such as connection to the internet, depreciation of computers, electricity and phone are already included in 'business as usual'.

Licences to use web-conferencing, VoIP or instant messaging software vary from nil to perhaps £5 per seat per month in a large enterprise.

Online meetings can achieve more

Compared with being face-to-face, online meetings often add extra value:

- Automatic tracking of time and levels of participation.

- You can go online 'at the drop of a hat'.

- You can use records of meetings to share ideas and decisions and how they were reached.

- Most conferencing tools are adaptable for very large or very small group meetings.

The facts

Very few wish to be an early adopter, so it may be reassuring to review some of the headlines emerging from research in 2009:

- Managers intend to make greater use of alternative meeting methods in the months ahead, including webinars (54 percent), teleconferencing (48 percent), and videoconferencing (30 percent).

- A survey of nearly 1000 people in the UK showed 70% of corporate organisers and 64% of intermediary agencies predict a growth in virtual conferences and a reduction in face-to-face events in the coming year.

- 56% of corporate buyers and 59% of intermediary agencies forecast fewer live events.

- Only 7% of corporates predicted an increase in face-to-face events in 2010.

- ABM and Forrester, in April 2009, reported that: "75% of business decision-makers attended three or more web-based events during the past 12 months".

And finally (travel agents look away now):

- In February 2009, Gartner predicted that high definition-based video meetings would replace 2.1 million airline seats annually by 2012, saving US$3.5 billion in travel and hospitality.

2

Re-think your meetings

The average business professional in the USA attends more than two meetings a day. Nine out of ten participants admit to daydreaming, 73% have brought other work to meetings and 39% say they have dozed off.

One firm reported that 80% of top management time was taken up discussing issues that account for less than 20% of the company's long term value. Psychologists found that the effectiveness of meetings influenced the well-being of employees and their attitude towards work.

So it seems like a good idea for companies to get better at meetings. As we shift to holding more meetings online, this provides a useful opportunity for a rethink.

Is a meeting really necessary?

The first question to ask is do we really need a meeting? Do you really need people to interact with one another to share opinions and knowledge, and build a shared picture of the issue under discussion?

If so, then a meeting should be ideal, but only assuming it is well run. In most cases where we need to share information, an e-mail will probably suffice. Busy people cannot afford to waste time in chit-chat or admiring reports the primary purpose of which is to bolster someone's self-esteem.

National Economic Council director Larry Summers nods off during a meeting with credit-card-industry CEOs. Source: Getty Images

A productive meeting must have a clear purpose and objective measures of success.

Beyond laundry lists

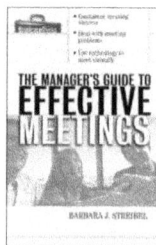

In her book *The Manager's Guide to Effective Meetings* (McGraw-Hill, 2002), Barbara Streibel says: "If I'm organizing a meeting, I want to get beyond 'discuss'. Maybe 'discuss and decide'. Or 'discuss and build a plan', or 'discuss and identify key barriers to success'. I want an action. I don't need a laundry list of what's happened in the last week."

We all know our meetings could be more efficient than they are. Here are some suggestions to get us started.

Fifteen practical hints to make meetings more effective, online or not

1. Break the superstitious habit; meet only for defined purposes.

2. Build a time-sensitive agenda and distribute it in advance.

3. Make sure you get all the right people to attend, but stick at that.

4. Allow participants to do as much pre-work as they can in advance.

5. Don't force people to stay on if the meeting has moved on to matters that don't concern them. (In an online meeting this can be accomplished much more easily.)

6. Don't tolerate digressions, ego-trips or time-stealers.

7. Gather and share feedback and use it to become better at running or taking part in meetings.

8. Record and distribute minutes for each meeting.

9. Break into small groups for problem-solving.

10. Before meeting, send out relevant information by email.

11. Apply agreed rules to govern how people should behave.

12. Use the correct tools and methods for brainstorming, categorising, voting/prioritising, group decision-making, surveys, action plans and meeting documentation.

13. Start and end meetings on time.

14. Don't let meetings drag on for too long - if necessary, break the work into a series of shorter meetings. (Again, this is much easier to do online because there hasn't been the need to travel to a central location.)

15. Set a periodic meetings-free day - perhaps even a week.

3

Select the tool for the job

What are your options?

Instant messaging is a form of real-time, online communication between two or more people based, originally, on typed text, but now extended to include the use of online audio and video. Instant messaging programs include Windows Live Messenger, Google Talk, IBM Lotus Sametime and Skype.

Web conferencing is used to conduct live meetings, training sessions or presentations via the internet. The extended functionality of web conferencing usually requires participants to download a special client application to their computers. Web conferencing incorporates a host of features, including online audio and video, application sharing, electronic whiteboards, shared media (such as PowerPoint presentations), text chat and polling. Web conferencing systems include Cisco WebEx, Microsoft LiveMeeting, Adobe Acrobat Connect and Citrix GoTo Meeting.

Video conferencing uses digital telecommunications to support remote meetings that employ both audio and video. Typically video conferencing takes place in a special facility rather than at the desktop, so it is often reserved for more senior management. The boundary between what can be achieved with video conferencing and with simpler instant messaging and web conferencing systems is

Top-end video conferencing, like this Cisco Telepresence system, requires access to a special facility, but provides as realistic an experience as you could wish for.

increasingly blurred, although 'telepresence' systems, that provide a highly authentic, high-definition interface are still very much at the top end.

It is quite common for an organisation to already possess the tools that they need, but for many people (particularly those outside IT) to know nothing about them, let alone how to use them. In some cases, employees have been trained in how to work the controls but have not been equipped with the behavioural skills they need, and have no idea what processes and procedures to follow.

Choosing the tool

Selecting the right tool depends a great deal on what you need people to do together:

- Brainstorming?
- Classifying?
- Voting / prioritising?

- Reaching group decisions?
- Participating in surveys?
- Action planning?
- Documenting outcomes?

The decision also depends on the numbers involved, the access participants are likely to have to the particular tools and technologies, and how important it will be for them to have a quiet space in which to participate.

Consider the level of fidelity that you will need. With a high fidelity system, participants will almost feel they are in the same room. With a low fidelity system, the experience will be not much better than a telephone conference. Pitch too low and your online sessions may not achieve their objectives. Pitch too high and you'll be consuming lots of unnecessary resources.

A meeting is more than an event

As you start to plan your meeting, it may help to divide the knowledge and information that relate to the subject of the meeting into four categories:

1. Information that participants can read and review on their own.

2. Information that benefits from listening and questioning a subject matter expert.

3. Information that needs to be discussed and then acted upon through joint problem-solving and decision-making.

4. Information that needs to be reviewed in depth, following an initial exposure.

Knowing the type of information you have allows you to start constructing your virtual meeting into a series of segments, including pre-work and post-work. Only items 2 and 3 in the list above need be addressed in detail during the meeting itself.

Think of the virtual meeting as an interactive moment in time, preceded by advance preparation and information sharing, and followed by continued reflection and action. Then you come upon the realisation that the tool you need is not just a place to talk and share content, but also a recording system, a dynamic notebook, a library, a gateway to other resources, a think-tank, a classroom, a reference tool and a virtual water cooler.

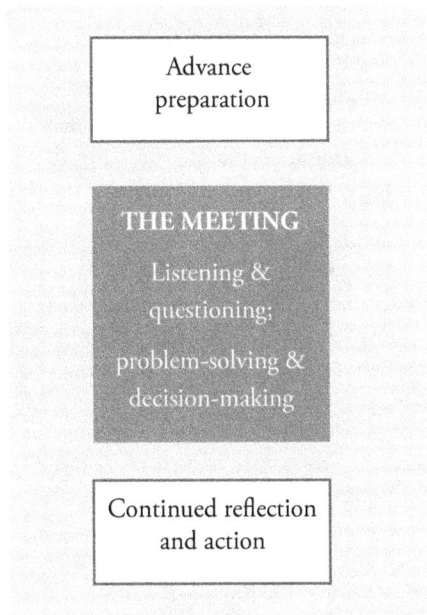

Advance preparation

THE MEETING

Listening & questioning;

problem-solving & decision-making

Continued reflection and action

4

Persuade the doubters

Socrates and Barack Obama – two unlikely technobobes

History repeating itself

In 2010, President Obama made his famously technophobic pronouncement that "With iPods and iPads and Xboxes and PlayStations – none of which I know how to work – information becomes a distraction, a diversion, a form of entertainment, rather than a tool of empowerment." In saying this, Obama joined a long tradition of grumbling about new technologies and new forms of media.

Apparently, Socrates objected to the spread of writing because it would lead to people relying on written texts rather than their memory (the irony being that we only know about this because his student, Plato, wrote it down). Moving on, in 1790 Enos Hitchcock was concerned about the increasing prevalence of romantic novels, proclaiming that "The free access which many young people have to romances, novels and plays has poisoned the mind and corrupted the morals of many a promising youth." Cinema was denounced

as 'an evil pure and simple' in 1910; comic books were said to lead children into delinquency in 1954; rock'n'roll was accused of turning the young into 'devil worshippers' in 1956; and Hillary Clinton attacked video games for 'stealing the innocence of our children' in 2005.

Author Douglas Admas pointed out that "anything invented after you're thirty is against the natural order of things and the beginning of the end of civilisation as we know it, until it's been around for about ten years, when it gradually turns out to be alright really. Apply this to movies, TV, rock music, punk, computers, the internet, mobile phones and social networking to work out how old you are."

Perhaps if we took a bit more notice of history, then we would be less inclined to repeat its mistakes.

Removing the mystique

For those who have no experience of them, online meetings may be surrounded by an air of mystique that is fuelled by quite strongly prejudicial views. Some of that negativity comes from fear of change, some from a poor previous experience and some from simply not knowing what an online meeting is like.

One obvious solution is to explain what real-time online communication is all about. Being 'real-time' requires all participants to be available at the same time; it's live, rather than self-paced. To be 'online' implies a state of connectivity, typically through a device such as a computer that is connected to the internet. Online communication is most obviously contrasted with being face-to-face, or using traditional media, such as print publications, tapes, CDs, radio and TV (all 'offline media').

Being between a rock and a hard place

When you ask people to meet online for the first time, you are asking them to adopt a way of working that they may regard as innovative and unproven. You may meet boundless enthusiasm, but you are almost bound to meet some resistance. Some will see the two words 'meet' and 'online' as a contradiction in terms.

When they are managing the introduction of new things, many people use a well-known model that is described in a book by Geoffrey Moore. He speaks of 'crossing the chasm' between the first 2.5% to take up a new idea or technology, whom he calls 'innovators', and the next group – the 13.5% whom he calls 'early adopters'.

Crossing your own particular chasm

You are likely to run into a number of barriers before you can say the project to introduce online meetings has crossed the chasm.

Managerial commitment:
You may struggle to win support for online meetings without the involvement of senior line management. They are likely to be most interested in the statistical evidence, so it is useful, if you are the person who is driving the change, to hold briefings and provide regular reports, detailing all the savings made and any other hard evidence.

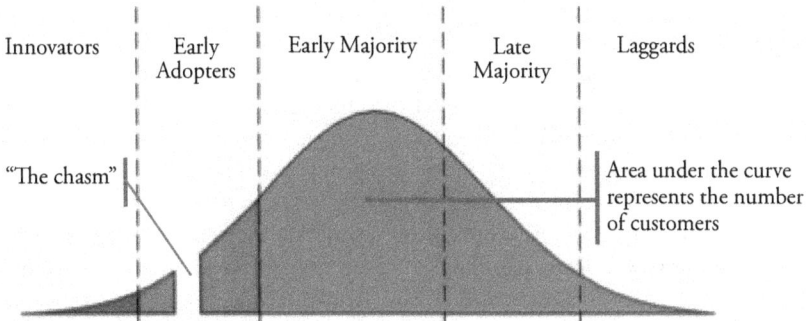

| Innovators | Early Adopters | Early Majority | Late Majority | Laggards |

"The chasm"

Area under the curve represents the number of customers

The Technology Adoption Lifecycle from Crossing the Chasm by Geoffrey Moore. Harper Business; Rev. 1999

Who	Attracted by	Put off by	Tactics	Timeline
Top managers	Cost saving Forward thinking Ownership of content	Cost Risk Lack of early action	Make them part of the project	Throughout
Co-support functions	Online meetings will help us all	Online meetings compete for resources or attention		Any time through the project
Other projects	This project will help us	The project competes for resources or attention	Seek linkages and synergy	Any time through the project
Senior line management	This meets a business need	It takes time to do	Meetings Briefings	Three months prior to launch
First line management	I may not need to pass on briefings to my people second hand	It takes time to do I have to manage it	Briefings from senior management Help desk	One month prior to launch
People who attend meetings	I can meet anyone, whenever and wherever I want	Lack of social interaction Techno fear	Ad campaign Personal tution	Two weeks prior to launch
Trainers	I am involved	I am not involved Will online meetings put me out of a job?	Integrate into the project	From the start

Technical commitment:

You'll need to 'do your sums'. Estimate the benefits in comparison with conventional meetings and other potential investments in business improvement. Find the most influential sponsor you can. You may need to sell online meetings as a leading edge project, or play it down according to the culture of your organisation. It is essential to create the conditions in which IT support is behind what you are trying to do.

User commitment:

You must provide a satisfying experience and may even have to provide rewards (tangible and intangible) to encourage people to take part. You'll need to ensure the system is accessible and easily available tand that everyone has the support they need to get up and running quickly. Look for local champions who can act as advocates. It may sound like a paradox, but try to maintain personal contact with them face-to-face and not just online.

Adoption strategies

Back in 1986, American academic Diane Dormant presented her *ABCDs of Managing Change*, which can help in recognising the stages that people pass through as they move towards trust and support for online meetings:

Stage 1 - Ignorance

At first people don't know what they don't know. They are indifferent to the use of online meetings because they have no knowledge of them. You need to take a leaf from the book of the advertising professional – do not go too deeply into logical argument or persuasion. Expose people to intriguing messages, slogans and eye-catching statistics. Be brief, be lively and positive. Try viral marketing using the full range of social media available to you. Publish good news stories and act as champion to pass on messages about new methods of meeting that will resonate with those who hear them.

> In Stage 3, people will move on from "how does this affect me?" to "go on then, show me"

Stage 2 - Anxiety

A raised level of awareness won't stop people from fretting over how online meetings will affect them personally. Will they encounter technical difficulties and waste valuable time dealing with problems? Will the system crash? Will they look foolish in front of their colleagues or managers? Will they find it difficult to convey important information if the participants are not physically present?

Now you need to take on the personality of a counsellor, reassuring participants with honest and authentic facts. Respond with sympathy, or pre-empt real fears by revisiting all the positive benefits of meeting online. If you are introducing online meetings as an enterprise-wide change, then you might think of giving vent to concerns through focus groups, road shows or online forums, in which you can gather and respond to questions, concerns and misapprehensions.

Stage 3 - Curiosity

As long as you continue to answer questions in a cool, calm and open manner, people will move on from "how does this affect me?" to "go on then, show me". This is an important shift from a position of self-protection to accepting that there really is going to be a change in how they do meetings.

As the champion, you must now explain the process, features and benefits of online meetings in some detail. You might put together some case material, perhaps in the form of a video interview with trusted colleagues who have already piloted the change.

As soon as it's available you should use qualitative data about the results of meeting online. Demonstrate how technologies like web conferencing can reduce time spent in meetings while increasing the amount of useful information that a participant can process, as well as make meetings more dynamic and focused. Show it as more inclusive, more flexible, accessible and effective, and participants will soon be ready to try it out for themselves.

Stage 4 - Readiness

Even when people are ready to take part themselves, they may still be unsure about how their own colleagues or managers will react to what they are doing. Now you become a combination of trainer and coach, teaching people what they need to know in order to participate, how to deal with resistance and how to derive maximum benefit from meeting online. As they learn from one another, participants will themselves become advocates and fend off the 'nay sayers'. Look out for positive shifts in attitude due to emerging results, and make capital of them.

Stage 5 - Acceptance

Ready, willing and able to use the new methods of meeting, participants will now begin to enjoy the personal benefits. You may be hearing technical or procedural questions, or the exchange of suggestions for improvement. Now, as people relax, your role is one of implementer, introducing more challenging or more ambitious activities that fully exploit the new methodology.

> "We're only just beginning to find out what it takes to make online meetings a success"

An approach of 'continuous performance improvement' begins to permeate the project. Listen for and act upon ideas for modifying materials and procedures, ensure any defects are fixed and watch as the technology becomes ever more integrated with the personalities and preferences of users.

Stage 6 - Fatigue

As people become regular and practised users, they may experience a mood of boredom or dissatisfaction. The sense of novelty and innovation has faded and they want greater challenge, more variety or more ambitious forms of interaction.

At this stage you pass into your ultimate role of maintainer. Keep everything fresh and up-to-date – the manuals, the reusable items such as welcome slides, action plans and agendas, and the success stories – otherwise disillusionment will set in. Encourage participants to express their own suggestions and assure them that they will be shared and given consideration.

Above all, each link must be reinforced between the newly-adopted methods of meeting and the goals of the organisation. No-one should stop striving for other, even more effective and innovative ways of reaching those goals.

Remember that this is a new medium and that we're only just beginning to find out what it takes to make online meetings a success. The chances are that, as new and innovative tools are developed and smart new ways of working with them, we will adapt this new medium to be much more successful than its predecessors.

Cultural differences

In 2004 a study of executives from 303 companies concluded that the best meetings involve lots of sharing of documents and visual information. The greatest productivity comes not from presenting and reviewing data, but from having everyone on the same page working towards a common goal.

Online meeting tools do this very well, but the British seem to take to it better than their French and German counterparts. UK business managers said they thought viewing documents together was the greatest benefit in driving productivity, whereas French and German managers rated being able to see facial expression. Unfortunately, even using webcams it is hard to pick up body language and facial movements accurately – for this you really do need a top-end telepresence system. However, with a little knowledge, skill and practice you can use a variety of features and techniques in a virtual meeting to pick up mood and motives.

But we are not recommending that you go online to socialise or meet new people for the first time. Our opening premise was that online meetings will save you from ruin at times when it is not possible to meet in the conventional way. In fact we can do a lot better than that as we begin to apply a myriad of useful tricks and techniques that you help you in building rapport and a team-working spirit, even when online.

5

Plan your meeting

Know your audience

Before you can begin to plan your meeting, you need to have a cleat picture of who the participants are going to be:

- How many are they and where are they based? Bear in mind that, if your participants are based in widely differing time zones, it can be difficult to find a time that suits everyone.

- How motivated are they likely to be to participate in this meeting?

- What prior knowledge or information do they already have?

- How independent are they as thinkers and decision-makers?

- What is the level of their authority and influence?

- How comfortable are they with the use of web-based tools?

- Have they been trained in how to use the online meetings tool?

- What are the existing relationships amongst the participants?

- What questions might they have, and can you collect them in advance?

- How well do they work together collaboratively?

- How freely are they likely to discuss issues that arise?

It is important to find out as much as you can about the people who will be participating in the meeting before you plan your session

Web conferencing software does not constrain you in terms of how you interact any more than a physical meeting room does. The software provides you with opportunities, as well as some constraints, but it does not determine the structure or balance of your meeting – that's down to you. Although it may not seem like this to start with, the fact that you're online is just a change of medium; the rules for successful meetings still apply just as they would face-to-face.

Whatever strategy you have for your session, some preparation is vital. You'll want to establish goals, set an agenda, plan what you're going to say, prepare visual aids, think about any practical activities, polls and other interactions, as well as allocate roles to those who will be helping you to run the meeting.

A typical virtual meeting will last between 30 and 90 minutes. It's the facilitator's job to remind people of the time and point out when the conversation goes off track.

How long and for how many?

A typical virtual meeting will last between 30 and 90 minutes; go beyond this and you will find it hard to maintain attention and energy levels. If you need to cover a lot of ground on a single day, run a number of short sessions interspersed with breaks in which actions can be completed offline.

Without experience, it can be hard to judge just how much to cover in a single meeting. If in doubt, err on the side of too little rather than too much: if you try to cover too much ground, you'll just cause overload; if you finish ahead of schedule, you allow everyone to get on with something else!

It's up to you just how much of your meeting plan you commit to paper in advance. If you're a less experienced facilitator, then you'll probably benefit from a detailed outline, which clearly explains who will do what and when, and for how long. You may choose to write out some of the things you intend to say on a word-for-word basis, even if just your opening comments.

As for how many to invite, a good rule of thumb is to have no more than 75% of the number of people you'd seat at a face-to-face meeting, assuming you want to achieve some meaningful outcomes and have everyone fully engaged.

Groups of more than twelve people invariably split into closely-knit pairs or threesomes, and that means more than one unofficial leader emerges.

People need sufficient time to reflect, explain and justify their thinking. The more people in the group, the longer it takes to reach understanding and give feedback.

The role of the facilitator

The person who takes on the role of facilitator is responsible for guiding participants toward the desired outcomes by following the agenda. This is, of course, the same role as the chair of a face-to-face meeting.

Good meeting planning is the first step towards a successful meeting, but facilitators will use many techniques to keep the meeting moving, to include everyone in the conversation, and to handle difficult situations.

First, facilitators need to run through the agenda and any special tools they are planning to use. They make sure ideas and proposals are not lost. They remind people of the time and point out when the conversation gets off track.

Often the team or project leader is the one who facilitates the meetings. Although they may not think of themselves as the facilitator, they should be attentive to the process of the meeting as well as the content. Even meeting participants can act in facilitative ways by asking questions or making a suggestions to get the meeting back on track or to draw out a person's ideas.

When you set up your meeting, pay attention to who will be in the chair and who else will be supporting. Bear in mind that most online meeting tools require you to define in advance the privileges that belong to different roles. You would not want all participants to have the freedom to interfere with your data, your slides or your agenda for example, nor would you want to enable 30 people all to speak at once.

The setting of privileges allows you to restrict who can speak and when, who can set up a new meeting space, who can annotate a slide or whiteboard or load a new document for sharing.

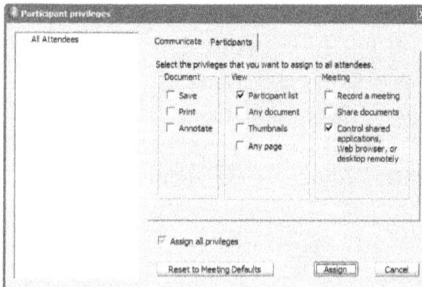

Defining privileges for participants in WebEx Meeting Center

These considerations are part of the process of setting up an online meeting just as, when you are face-to-face, you have to check you have the right number of chairs, the projector works and there are enough coffee and biscuits.

Getting some help

If you are working with an unusually large group, the topic is complex, the agenda is unlike any you've managed before or you are relatively inexperienced as a facilitator, consider working with an assistant.

The assistant is generally not as concerned with the detail of the online meeting; their job is to make sure you can concentrate on your role as process facilitator, by making sure the session runs smoothly.

The assistant may welcome participants as they log in, handle any technical questions and problems, provide quick, holding responses to messages in the text chat, load presentations and launch polls, breakout rooms and shared applications. You could also use them to act as scribe on the whiteboard. The assistant does not need to be an expensive resource, but could prove invaluable when you need your mind to be clear to concentrate on the issues of the meeting.

Alternatively, consider spreading the load with one or more other facilitators, or handing over specific tasks to participants who are experienced at meeting online, who have the capability to help with a task and know what is expected.

Establishing goals

Any meeting should have a clear business purpose. But the meeting also represents an opportunity to reinforce the values that the organisation aspires to with regard to the way that employees treat one another. Without a clear understanding of purpose and values, you have no way of knowing whether or not an online meeting is an appropriate solution, what you should cover and what methods of interaction and recording you should use.

You can increase *engagement* and *satisfaction* by ensuring that the meeting is not just a passing on of information that could be handled better using email, web content or online documents. As we have said before, often the best approach is to combine a live online meeting with self-paced methods used before and after.

Why does a meeting need planning?

Planning is what you do to ensure that everything that should happen at a meeting, does happen. A meeting is an opportunity to let others know how we feel, what we want and what we need, and what we are thinking. We are not all equally good at communicating these things, and most of us can improve our skills. We adapt our preferred styles of communication according to who we are meeting and what we'd like to achieve. For example, negotiating will require a different approach to interrogating, persuading, cajoling, disciplining, etc.

Even when you are using webcams, it's more difficult to read body language than it is face-to-face.

Whenever we meet there is the possibility of misunderstanding. When we are face-to-face a change of mood is easy to spot, and most of us have a good bag of tricks to help to put a relationship back on kilter. It may be more difficult to do this online when body language is usually invisible and when what is said and what is written is so easily recorded for posterity. That is why a clear agenda, a good structure and some clear 'rules of engagement' are so useful.

Active listening when you are face-to-face is something you do with your eyes, your ears and through your own body language and comments. When you're online, you have to be even more sensitive to tone of voice, more tolerant of cryptic and ambiguous text messages, and more watchful for signs that a participant may have dropped out. As facilitator, you need to be aware of all the available communication channels and make sure they are neither overly restricted or abused. That's worth thinking through in advance, rather than just 'winging it' on the day.

What should a plan include?

Your online meeting plan may include not only the agenda, but prompts to remind you what to do and say to keep the meeting on track, make sure everyone participates, and reach the goals that were set for the meeting.

What you decide will set the tone and culture for the meeting as democratic or controlling, competitive or collaborative. It will ensure that the meeting is be conducted in harmony with the culture of your organisation.

The agenda for a meeting does not usually explain *how* the meeting is to be run. Typically, it lists the topics to be discussed, the time to be allocated to each topic and the names of those who will be contributing. In the design of an online meeting you may also want to set out how opinions will be shared and decisions made using the various tools available.

Once you have found the most successful format for your online meetings, you can call upon a set of familiar tools and regular techniques that you know have worked before. By this stage your planning can be as routine and straightforward as it would be for a face-to-face meeting.

Structuring the session

Do not underestimate the need for introductions at the start of an online meeting. This is most effectively accomplished using voice, which establishes a more personal and informal tone.

A welcome slide showing the purpose of the meeting, start and finish times and a photo of the facilitator.

A screen capture of the interface to your system, showing where to find the most commonly-used tools

An ice-breaker slide which allows participants to show where they are currently in the world

For people who join early, and who are not practised with the system you are using, you could provide a simple activity to get them used to the various tools. A common ice-breaker is to use a map of your country or of the world upon which participants can indicate their location using the markup tools.

And always display a welcome slide with the meeting title and objective, the start and finish times, and the facilitator's name and photo.

To help any participants who are new to the system you are using, you could keep on hand a slide that shows a screen capture of the interface, with the tools you are most likely to be using in the meeting clearly labelled.

Present the ground rules, the expected outcomes and the agenda. You might also like to include an activity early on in the proceedings which gets participants using the text chat, so they will feel comfortable using this facility throughout the meeting.

If you are unsure where your participants will stand relative to the topic you are presenting, consider including an activity early on such as a poll. This will quickly provide you with the information you need to tailor the meeting to meet the characteristics of the participants.

6

Use media to engage and inform

Using voice

Body language provides an important channel of communication at a conventional meeting. Don't try to overcompensate for its absence by turning your online meeting into a production number – rarely do people come to a meeting looking to be entertained.

Nevertheless, audio will be ever-present and must deliver the major part of your message. This shouldn't represent a problem, because it is possible to communicate very successfully using sound as the principle medium, without eye contact or body language, as has been demonstrated successfully for many decades by the radio.

It is important to obtain the best possible audio quality, as this has an important effect on how participants perceive the quality of the meeting as a whole. So make sure you have a reliable broadband connection and use a good quality headset or mic.

Check before you start the session that your mic is set to the correct volume, neither so soft that you are hard to hear, nor so loud that you are distorted.

Look directly into the camera if you want to establish eye contact with other participants

Using live video

Many web conferencing systems make it possible to provide a live video feed from the facilitator's webcam, which is typically shown in a small window. Some systems also make it possible to show live video feeds of participants. Live video can make a useful contribution, but using it throughout a session can be very distracting. If you want participants to concentrate their attention on a slide, whiteboard exercise or some other visual element, then a simultaneous video feed will get in the way.

A short, live video introduction by the facilitator will help to reduce some of the remoteness participants might feel online. But it isn't necessary to continue providing video, because those initial few seconds will create a long-lasting image.

Live video can also be useful in question and answer sessions to show the expert as they give their responses.

Ideally, you should look directly into the camera to establish eye contact. This may prove quite a strain if you're not a professional TV presenter, which is another good reason for you to keep your use of video to short bursts.

And listening on video can be at least as good as speaking. When participants are talking, use body language, such as eye contacts and nods, to show that you are listening.

It also pays to make sure that you are well lit and that the background shows your working environment as you would want it seen. And don't forget you're on camera! You wouldn't want to be caught picking your nose or worse.

Slides

Slides are not essential to every online meeting; you also have the ability to share applications, display documents, tour web sites, carry out whiteboard activities and conduct polls - all of which can act as the primary visual focus. However, slides can be extremely useful both as visual aids and as signposts, as long as they are used properly, avoiding the risk of the dreaded 'death by PowerPoint'.

Research shows that we can absorb and recall information better from words and pictures than from words alone, which is not surprising when you consider that the majority of our sensory input is visual. Pictures are powerful and they are memorable, but it does matter what pictures you use - different types of information require different types of visuals to convey meaning most clearly.

Consider some of the uses:

• Photos of yourself and other speakers.

• Diagrams to represent processes, principles, structures and layouts.

• Photos to represent actual people, events, and objects.

• Photos and illustrations to represent abstract concepts.

• Screen grabs to show software applications.

• Charts to represent numeric data.

Audio is likely to be your primary verbal channel, so don't confuse the participant with a second verbal channel in the form of text on the screen. The participant won't know whether to listen or read; and because they can do the latter much faster than the former, they'll probably tune out what you're saying.

Use text on slides sparingly, for example:

• The agenda.

• Titles, which signpost the current topic.

• Anything the participant might want to make a note of, such as terms, URLs, names or quotes.

• Labels for diagrams, photos or charts.

• Lists, bulleted or numbered, but only in moderation.

Summary

Use images for clarity and memorability
Use the right types of images for the job
Avoid gratuitous images
Keep images clear and simple

Lists work well in moderation and do focus attention on one point at a time. However, present the list point-by-point rather than all at once

Note that when you are presenting items in a list, it is not good practice to show those items that you are yet to cover – reveal these in subsequent slides. And don't be tempted to use your bullets as a script – as an online presenter, if you really do need a script, you can have this in front of you in paper format, or in a separate window.

If you have to present a lot of text, distribute this as a separate document, or provide a link to materials to be read before or after the session.

Be careful when re-using slides which you normally use in a live presentation. Your slides are likely to be displayed in a smaller window and may degrade in quality when they are converted to the system's own format. The best solution is to keep them simple and bold.

You should also be prepared for the possibility that your transitions and animations will not be reproduced faithfully, if at all, by the system. This could mean you have to reconstruct any slide builds as a sequence across a number of slides. This can be quite easily accomplished in PowerPoint by making copies of the slide which contains all the items in the build and then selectively removing items so that one more appears with each successive slide.

Sharing documents

Many systems will allow you to upload and share a file such as a Word document, Excel spreadsheet or PDF. If you need to present detailed information that would not convert well into PowerPoint slides, then this represents a useful option. A big plus is that you can talk through the document and highlight particular sections as you go using the markup tools. What you will not be able to do is edit the document – for that you need application sharing (see the next section).

Beware of overdoing the amount of information that you present this way. In-depth reading of documents is something usually better carried out individually, before or after the session.

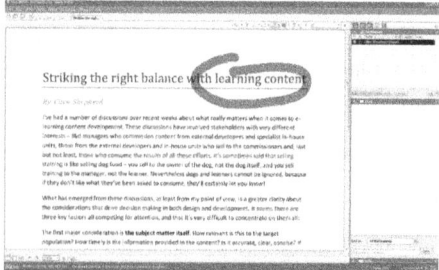

You can upload and share files such as Word documents and spreadsheets and then use the markup tools to highlight particular sections

www.onlignment.com

Playing back multimedia materials and web content

If you are confident that all participants will have reasonable bandwidth available, you can share web pages with them, including all forms of embedded content such as video and Flash animations. Typically, all you will have to do is type or copy in the URL (web address) for the web page you want to share.

Watching a long video is not a great use of meeting time, so consider asking participants to do this before or after the

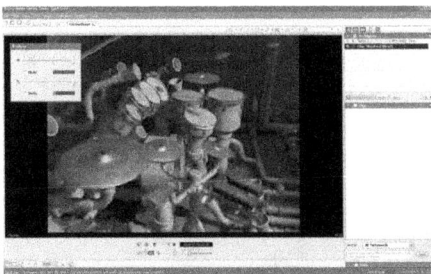

Some systems allow you to present multimedia material, such as audio and video

session. On the other hand, a short and engaging burst of multimedia content might just provide the inspiration you need for the next activity in your meeting.

7

Use interaction to solve problems and make decisions

Assume distractions

If you thought people could be distracted in a real meeting, then consider how much more scope there is for them to tune out when you're working online. Events happening around them, constant interruptions, and the easy availability of alternative things to do on their computers, often take the focus of attention away from the screen. With the participants largely invisible, even if each person is actively engaged, how are you to know? Without regular interactivity, you are flying blind, you are just hoping for the best. Interactivity proves that communication is taking place.

Luckily, web conferencing systems provide a host of very usable interactive devices, from simple text chat, through to virtual whiteboards, breakout rooms and application sharing. Let's take a look:

Text chat

The chat facility typically operates alongside the virtual meeting and is available for use at any time. Participants can use it to ask or answer questions or as a 'back channel' to pass public or private notes. Some facilitators may find this activity a little strange – after all, we would probably feel uncomfortable if people seated around a table passed messages to one other during a meeting. However, many participants find this channel of great use: they exchange contact details, links, thoughts and comments; they help to move the meeting along, without intervention by the facilitator.

Chat is a good option for questions requiring brief, open-ended responses. If you don't want participants to 'cheat' by borrowing the opinions of the last person, ask participants to type in their comments but not press 'send' until told to.

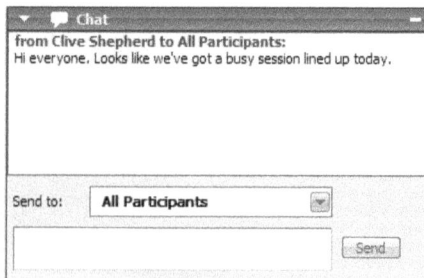

> ▾ 💬 Chat — ▬
> from Clive Shepherd to All Participants:
> Hi everyone. Looks like we've got a busy session lined up today.
>
> Send to: All Participants   ▾
>
> [   ] Send

| Hand | Yes | No |

Ticks and crosses

Some systems provide a way for facilitators to obtain simple yes/no responses from participants, totalling up the responses automatically. Facilitators can use this mechanism to obtain confirmations ('Can you hear me clearly?', 'Shall I move on?') or to conduct simple polls ('Have you used this system before?', 'Do you agree with this?').

Voice interaction

Participant audio is the best option for longer, open-ended responses (or questions) that would require too much typing to express in chat.

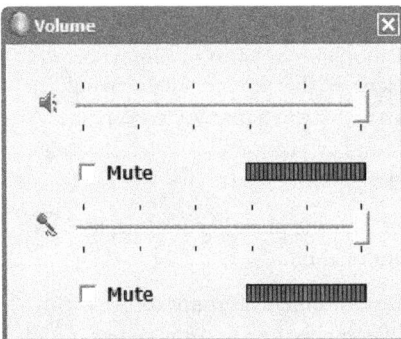

Your job will be made much easier if participants mute their own mics when they're not speaking. However, sometimes you'll need to take control of who speaks and when

The advantages of using voice are obvious: the communication is more natural and spontaneous, and there is no need for typing. However, some moderation is required to avoid everyone speaking at once. Most systems use a 'hands-up' facility, which allows participants to signify that they want to speak. It is then up to the facilitator to 'turn the mic on' or otherwise allow the participant to speak.

Whiteboard

In the context of web conferencing, a whiteboard is a blank screen or a prepared slide, on to which participants can draw or type. Whatever is placed on the whiteboard can be seen by all participants. You can use whiteboards in a wide variety of ways:

• for ice-breaking activities ('Indicate on this map where you are located');

• for capturing expectations at the beginning of a session and then revisiting them at the end;

• for listing participants' ideas, flip chart-style ('Where should we hold our sales convention this year?');

• for assessing how things are going ('Draw a picture showing how you're feeling about this topic');

• for structured questions ('What are you hoping to gain from this meeting?');

• as a place where participants can paste screen shots from an application on their computer, including elements of documents, spreadsheets and web pages.

Our top five ideas	
TERRY	CHRISTENE
SOLVEIG	MIA

To avoid everyone writing on top of each other, you can segment the whiteboard so each participant has their own space

Question
How often do you participate in online meetings?
Answers
○ Frequently
○ Fairly often
○ Occasionally
○ Seldom
○ Never

The polling facility allows you to survey the opinion of all participants simultaneously. This is a particularly useful feature if you are running a large meeting and need to find ourt more about the audience or take a vote.

To avoid everyone typing or drawing on top of each other, the facilitator can prepare a slide with sections allocated to each of the participants.

Instead of having participants type their responses, consider encouraging them to draw pictures instead.

Whiteboards can usually be archived for use after the session. If the system won't allow this, just make your own screen grab.

Polls

Polls allow you to ask multiple-choice and other types of questions in order to profile participants or to survey opinion. They are usually set up in advance, although most systems will allow you to modify or add new questions on the fly. An advantage of online polling is that you can obtain totalled-up responses instantly, allowing you to act immediately on the information.

Polls and surveys employed during a live session should be brief and advance the cause of the objectives for the meeting; otherwise they are better deployed separately, either before or after the session.

Breakout rooms

Some systems provide you with the facility to allocate participants to groups, have them then undertake activities in those groups in separate virtual 'rooms', monitor what is happening in each room, and then bring back the groups for a review in plenary. This process mirrors syndicate room activity in a physical conference suite and can be used for much the same purposes, for example:

• for strategic planning or obstacle elimination;

• to allow different groups to work with different content or using different tools (for example one might be doing SWOT analysis while another does a Force Field Analysis);

- if there are varying levels of seniority or functional expertise in a meeting, the session can be divided and different facilitators can moderate separate breakout rooms;

- participants can discuss different scenarios, using their own whiteboards to take notes;

- you can conduct a number of action learning sets in parallel.

With a smaller group, say two to five participants, audio can be used more freely than in plenary. If you want, a spokesperson from each group can report to the larger group once everyone has moved back into the main room.

You may need to use an assistant to help with the management. However responsibilities are divided, it is important for one of the facilitators to drop in regularly to provide guidance. It may pay to set up a template on each whiteboard in advance, to help direct the groups and get them started.

Until they become practised, participants at virtual meetings tend not to follow instructions very well. When put into a virtual breakout room, often they will wait for the meeting leader to show up to reissue instructions or manage the tools for them.

For participants who are 'becalmed' there is usually a device for sending a call to the meeting host who receives a text message asking for help.

Application and desktop sharing

All web conferencing systems allow a participant to share an application resident on their computer or to share a view of their entire system ('desktop sharing'). The control of the application or desktop can also be passed from participant to participant.

This feature has a number of important uses:

- You can view a document as a group and edit the content dynamically.

- You could share a diagram, such as a mind map or a Gantt chart and pass control from person to person to complete a task.

- You could demonstrate how to use a new software package and have participants take turns to try it out for themselves.

- You can display presentations without uploading them to the web conferencing system's own format. This ensures all the functionality of the original presentation is maintained.

The downside of application sharing is that it demands a fast broadband connection if it is not to appear jerky and disjointed.

It's a good idea to open the application before you need to use it, log in if necessary and set it up to show exactly what you want.

Find out how much space participants will have on their screens to view applications and then size your window accordingly. If

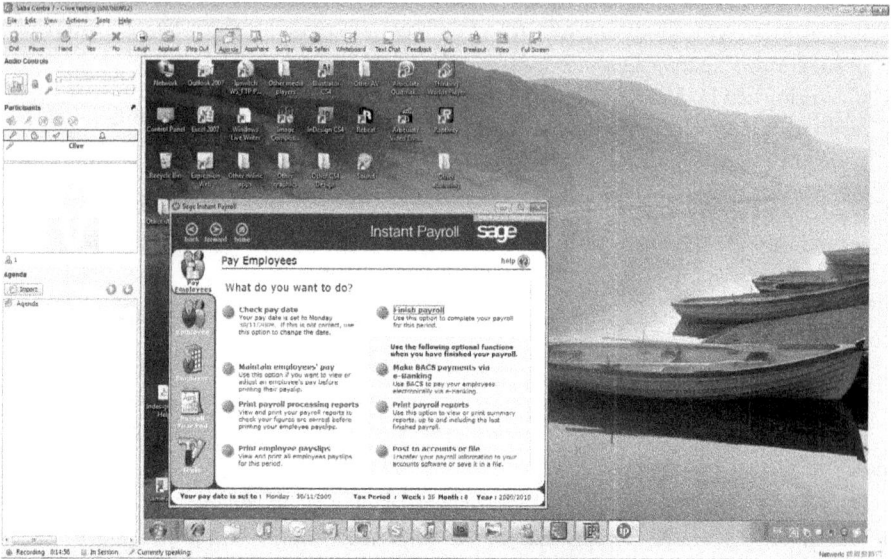

Application sharing allows facilitators to share single applications or, as in this case, a whole desktop.

your screen resolution is much higher than that of other participants, they will have to scroll to see the whole application window.

Make sure you close all other applications, especially instant messaging and email – you don't want embarrassing pop-ups to appear during your meeting!

Web tours

Some systems allow you to take all participants to a common web site and then allow them to interact with that site individually. This can be contrasted with application sharing using a browser, when all participants see the same view.

Web tours could be used to help familiarise participants with a new site. You could also

employ this facility to have participants interact with games, simulations, quizzes, questionnaires and all sorts of other web resources which would not normally be available directly within the system.

Web tours provide a way for a group to jointly explore a web resoource.

When to interact

Most experts agree that participants will lose concentration in a virtual meeting unless they are required to interact in some way every three to five minutes. It goes without saying that interactivity should not be used for its own sake. Each interaction should be meaningful and productive, and this requires planning and preparation.

Try to involve the whole group in the interaction. Serial participation (one person interacting after another) is rarely the best option as it takes too long.

It is better to focus on activities that can be undertaken in small groups or concurrently, using breakout rooms, polls, application sharing, chat or the whiteboard.

8

Manage the meeting

An experienced facilitator should be aware of how and why people react as they do in groups and know how to deal with the dynamics. They establish and maintain personal credibility because they:

- are prepared;

- obtain information about the participants, their accomplishments, behaviour and preferences in advance;

- manage the meeting environment sensibly;

- display effective communication and presentation skills;

- use questioning skills and techniques effectively;

- respond properly to all calls for clarification or feedback;

- provide positive reinforcement and motivational incentives for contributions at the meeting;

- evaluate the inputs and outcomes of the meeting;

- report and act upon evaluation information.

Pecking order

Yes it happens, not only with hens but also with other animals (including humans). A real or symbolic contest between two opponents determines who is allowed to 'peck' with whom. When a new member

With humans, as with hens, a pecking order will be established

joins, there is unrest until a new contest determines the new member's place in the group.

As long as the group is working out who's who, it gets in the way of settling down to work. If participants know nothing about each other, it is difficult for them to know where they stand in relation to each other. That is why a facilitator will always try to ensure people have been properly introduced to one another as early and as rapidly as possible. An obvious opportunity is some kind of round the (virtual) table introduction.

Something else for the facilitator to consider is the extent to which the group begins to feel and think alike. Behavioural norms will develop, and although usually unspoken, they may go as far as determining how much work will be done, when and by whom.

Getting to know everyone

As we've mentioned before, it's important to know as much as you can about who will be taking part in the meeting:

- their demographics – age, gender and so on;

- what prior knowledge they have of the topic of the meeting, what their attitudes might be to this topic, and what special knowledge, information or insights they might be able to bring along;

- any personal agendas, coloured by the demands and priorities of their particular jobs and careers;

- whether they have the confidence, intellect and authority to wrestle with a problem by themselves; or whether they prefer to use others as a sounding board and compare opposing arguments before reaching a conclusion;

- their attitude towards meeting online rather than face-to-face.

You cannot expect everyone to thrive in a free-form, exploratory, fast-moving process for reaching resolutions. Conversely, if you slow them down, the creative or spontaneous thinkers may withdraw. A great benefit of combining the session with self-paced activities, before and after, is that it plays to the stengths of each end of the spectrum.

> "You cannot expect everyone to thrive in a free-form, exploratory and fast-moving process"

Roles within groups

"Some", says the bard, "have greatness thrust upon them". Roles in a group may be actively chosen or thrust upon those who passively accept them under pressure or in the absence of other volunteers.

You may encounter any or all of the following roles in a group. Note that one person may assume more than one role. The first two are active roles (leaving aside the facilitator):

Workers:
Workers are an uncomfortable reminder of what all other members ought to achieve if only they tried. The role is taken on by one who is more intelligent or a higher performer than the others and not prepared to go at the pace of the slowest. Some in this role are driven to be best at everything.

Fighters:
Bolstered by the respect of the group for speaking their minds, fighters may take every chance to challenge or annoy the facilitator.

There are also passive roles:

Favourites:
Favourites usually communicate best. They seem to know everything about the other group members. Others confide in them. They are more likely to be seen guiding and counselling than assuming the role of leader.

Idiots:

Idiots struggle to work hard, but accomplish little. They respond by loudly entertaining or volunteering to do helpful jobs in order to win approval. When someone throws themselves enthusiastically into using mark-up tools to doodle across your slides or whiteboard, you know with whom you are dealing.

Conformists:

Conformists keep their heads down and may not challenge or defend a point of view. Usually they wait for the power struggle to end and then join the unofficial leader. They avoid confrontation. They may be consistently last to post a comment or opinion in the text chat.

Outsiders:

'Innocents' may be nudged into the position of outsider against their will. Typically introvert, they may have joined the group later than the others and have crossed boundaries they did not even know existed. A skilful facilitator should recognise these outsiders and tactfully help them back into the group.

'Mr Nasty' types become outsiders simply because they are unpleasant and create friction. Once exposed they are ostracised, and you are unlikely to succeed in bringing them back into the fold.

'Mr Superior' is high on intelligence but low on social and emotional skills. Always one step ahead and extremely arrogant, this person has no desire to form part of the group. 'Mr Superior' can create tension, interfere with motivation and productivity,

and spoil the atmosphere in a group. It is often best to address them through private chat, or contact them off-line and confront their destructive behaviour.

Scapegoats:

A group that feels frustrated by low challenge, or dominated by the facilitator, may punish the weakest member. Members try to empathise and suppress negative impulses like envy and rivalry. But when they need to let off steam, they may channel their energies into aggression. The spirit and structure of the group comes under threat and the weakest member of the group becomes a target. Sometimes the pressure is heavy and sustained.

How important is body language?

When you are face-to-face it may be easy to spot when someone is holding back from telling you how they are feeling. The harder they try to conceal their upset, worry, anger or even happiness, the more likely it is that their body and tone will reveal the truth.

This brings to mind the work of Albert Mehrabian. He believed that words, tone of voice and facial expression each influence how we feel about the person who is speaking, and the authenticity of their message.

His suggestion is that a listener will take non-verbal cues as a more reliable guide to underlying feelings, attitudes and motives than the actual words themselves. If the words are at odds with the tone of voice and facial expression, they tend to mistrust the speaker and disregard the words.

Be careful, because this is not the same same as oft-quoted but false assertion that only 7% of what a person says is communicated through words!

This is important because one of the most damaging arguments against meeting online is the misconception that you cannot get a message across if someone cannot see and hear you. This is a myth that has been well and truly busted.

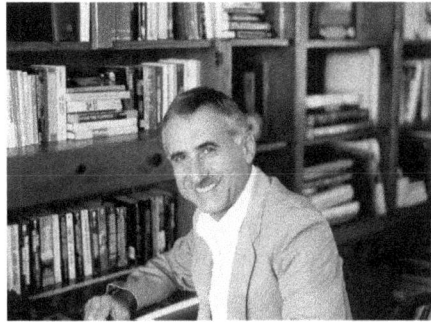

Albert Mehrabian

9

Keep a record of outputs

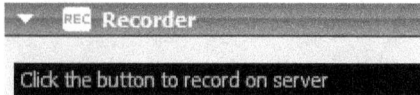

Recording the whole session

It is uncommon for an audio recording to be made of a face-to-face meeting (unless you have to make such a record for legal compliance, as in a police interview). When you are online, however, it is not unusual to make a complete recording of everything including audio, video, presentation materials and contemporaneous text chat.

If you do set the session to record, remember to let everyone know at the start that everything that happens will be saved and may be reviewed by others who are not present at the live meeting.

The session recording may be a very useful asset for someone who ought to have taken part but was unable to do so. However, for those who did take part, it is necessary to provide some more concise record of key decisions and actions.

Drawbacks of recordings

Being present at a live meeting has obvious advantages. You can affect the pace and direction of the meeting. You can ask and answer questions, make comments, share items on your desktop or on the Web, and take part in polls and surveys.

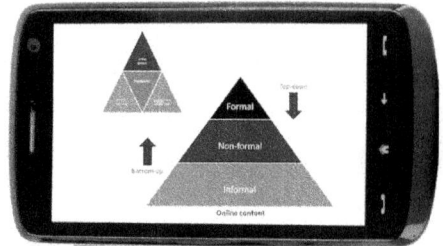

Presentations can be adapted to act as stand-alone resources in a number of ways. Pictured above are examples of an Articulate presentation, a slide show running as a movie on a mobile phone, and a presentation on SlideShare.

But, if your only access to the same meeting is via an archived recording, you soon come to regret the loss of those advantages.

What is more, those little dips in signal strength, slips of the tongue and minor errors that passed without comment in the live meeting, become an irritant in the recording. A live audience understands that you may need to cough or consult your notes, but everyone expects a recording to be of an agreeable standard.

It is rare for the recording of an online meeting to undergo any post-production work to tidy up the sequencing and optimise the sound quality. In some cases it is not technically possible to do this even if you had the time and motivation. Some systems save recordings in standard media formats so thay can be played in any media player. Others use proprietary formats that depend on the vendor's own media player. Often the audio is compressed to keep the files small, which means that what might have been poor quality sound in the first place is now further degraded.

In a live session you may sit through unnecessary instructions about how to use the web conferencing interface. You may be prepared to wait as everyone else catches up with polls and surveys. The person viewing the recording, on the other hand, can only passively observe these interactions and so is unlikely to keep engaged for the same period of time as they might have done in the live meeting.

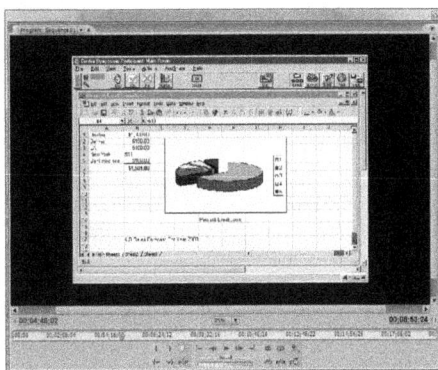

Depending on your system, it may be possible to edit the recording of your session using a video editing software

So what else can you do? Well, if some part of the meeting includes an important presentation then you could publish that in its native format such as PowerPoint.

You could also consider created a narrated PowerPoint presentation, using a plug-in such as Articulate or Adobe Presenter. This allows you to make make your points much more clearly and concisely than you can usually achieve live. And if you take care to label each slide and include notes, your audience can navigate easily to just the information they want.

Other ways to record outputs

In a virtual meeting, just as face-to-face, the recording of information can be achieved in various ways:

- People can take their own notes and optionally share and consolidate them at the end. This could be achieved online, using voice or text chat, but may also be carried out offline if preferred.

- You can appoint someone as a scribe who uses the text chat or (much better) a separate notes window to capture the key points from and for everyone.

- You can work together as a group to define the outputs in a way that lets people validate and verify what is noted.

By making the notes conspicuous, on a whiteboard that everyone can see, you gain some advantages:

- Participants have a place to focus their attention.

- Speakers can check how accurately their words have been understood and recorded.

- Whiteboards can be saved and then displayed again at the next meeting,

- The group can focus their thoughts more clearly when they can see their proposals and ideas in print.

- Participants will not be overwhelmed by the need to scan a large volume of text – some of which may be relevant and some of which may not.

- Participants will not be distracted by having to keep an eye on text appearing in the text chat at the expense of the task in hand.

- Whiteboards can be originated in a virtual break-out room and then presented in plenary.

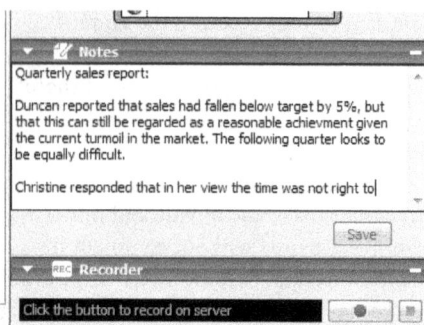

Some systems have special Notes panels, which can be used to record outputs from the meeting.

What should you note?

In a typical face-to-face meeting, the facilitator may designate separate flipcharts for action items, decisions, and the parking lot (issues to be addressed later). In a virtual meeting, you can achieve the same by preparing a whiteboard for each:

Action plan:
This is the place to record the items people have agreed to take responsibility for after the meeting. Be sure to record the action, who is responsible and a target deadline.

Decisions:
This records the agreements reached at the meeting, allowing all participants to confirm their understanding.

Parking lot:
The parking lot (sometimes known as 'the bin', 'the trap' or 'issues') is a place to record ideas, questions, or future agenda items. This helps to avoid subverting the agenda onto side issues by deferring them to another time.

Keeping minutes online

In some meetings, you will want to keep more detailed notes of the proceedings of the meeting in the form of minutes. With some systems you can achieve this using a special notes panel. Another option is for the minute taker to type into a standard word processing program and share this application when agreement is needed.

When keeping minutes:

- Record the main thrust of an idea.

- State the topic and the date of the meeting.

- Don't paraphrase or try to correct - use the speaker's own words where possible.

- Check with the speaker that what you've written reflects what they've said.

- Let all agree whether abbreviations and misspellings are acceptable.

- Type as fast as you can but ask the group to slow down if you fall behind, or nominate more than one note taker.

- If possible use bullets, numbers or contrasting colours to separate one point from another.

- At the end of the meeting, copy and paste the text into a document that can be more easily edited and distributed.

10

Follow up

In part nine we discussed the mechanics of recording both the content and the outcomes of your online meetings. We finish off by looking at what else you can do to keep people informed, engaged and feeling positive about their next online meeting.

Of course the greatest motivation is to reach a measurable accomplishment that has personal as well as organisational value. This is true of all meetings, and not just those that happen online. But running meetings online does have particular advantages, not least the fact that outputs and commitments can be so obvious and visible. It is hard to avoid an undertaking that is expressed openly in words that all can see. And if a meeting has been recorded, archived and then made freely available for review, no-one can ask to be excused on the grounds that they forgot what was intended.

Action planning

Ultimately it is the quality of the outcomes from a meeting that makes the biggest difference. One of the best ways to ensure that these outcomes are widely known and

acted upon is to draw up an action plan which lists the tasks to be accomplished and the people responsible for those tasks. The action plan can then be sent to all participants, along with a list of key decisions made and other important information recorded at the meeting.

An effective action plan will answer a series of simple yet vital questions:

1. What has to be done?

2. Why does this have to be done? What strategic goal is it supporting?

3. How will the action be carried out? What process will be followed?

4. Who will carry out the action and who will be accountable for ensuring the action is completed? These will not necessarily be the same people.

5. When should the action be completed? You might like to look at best and worst case scenarios.

6. How you will know when it's been accomplished – what will you be able to see, hear or read to indicate a successful outcome?

What	Why	How	Who	When	Indicators
The action	The goal it serves	The process	The person who is accountable	The target deadline	The measures of success

The action plan answers all the important questions

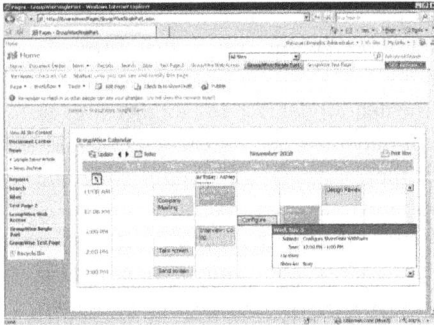

Tools like Microsoft Sharepoint can be used after the session to share files, continue discussions using forums, and collaborate on outputs using wikis

Continuing the discussion

Sometimes meetings seem to go on forever but, more often than not, they are not long enough to fully evaluate a problem or idea from all the necessary perspectives. This is where a balance must be struck between live communication (sometimes described as 'synchronous') and on-going, self-paced discussion ('asynchronous'). Synchronous communication, face-to-face or online, creates the impetus for the more thorough and reflective problem-solving and decision-making that follows.

Like its synchronous counterpart, asynchronous communication can be accomplished highly effectively online, without the need for costly travel. Here are some of the options:

- Email - not easy to control, particularly in terms of who sees what, but simple and ubiquitous, both on desktop computers and on mobile devices.

- Discussion forums - ideal when you want a record of the various contributions, easily accessible on the internet or your intranet.

- Wikis - which make it easy for a deliverable to be worked on by several people simultaneously. If this seems too wacky for you, then you could try collaborative tools like Google Docs.

- Ideal is a system that allows you to establish a group presence online and then share documents and continue discussions. This can be achieved using enterprise tools such as Microsoft Sharepoint or any number of inexpensive web-based tools.

Evaluating the meeting

While we are talking online tools, we should not forget surveys, not necessarily conducted during the meeting itself using the built-in polling tools, but more reflectively at some point after the meeting. Surveys are incredibly easy these days to set up and track online. You could create a link to the survey on the last slide of your meeting.

For some time to come, meeting online will be a relatively unusual experience for many participants. You really need to know how they felt about the experience: Was the pace right? Did any technical problems hinder them? Were they confortable with the management of the meeting? Did they have enough opportunity to convey their own thoughts and feelings? If you don't know the asnwers to these questions you risk repeating the same mistakes over and again.

And so ...

That concludes this quick tour of the essentials of effective online meetings. These are early days, so expect best practice to evolve, ingeneous new features to be added to the available systems, and even cleverer applications to be discovered by those, like you, who have to put these tools into practice.

On reflection you may feel that much of what we have discussed is old hat, because it applies equally well to face-to-face meetings. To some extent that is true, but we make no apologies for the fact. The majority of face-to-face meetings are not only inefficient, because they could be more economically conducted online, but ineffective, because they are so poorly facilitated. We can take this switch of media as an opportunity to rethink how and why we meet together in real-time, to make sure we are not condemned to endlessly repeat the mistakes of the past.

Here's to happy online meetings. Not too frequent, not too long, but great fun and highly productive while they last.

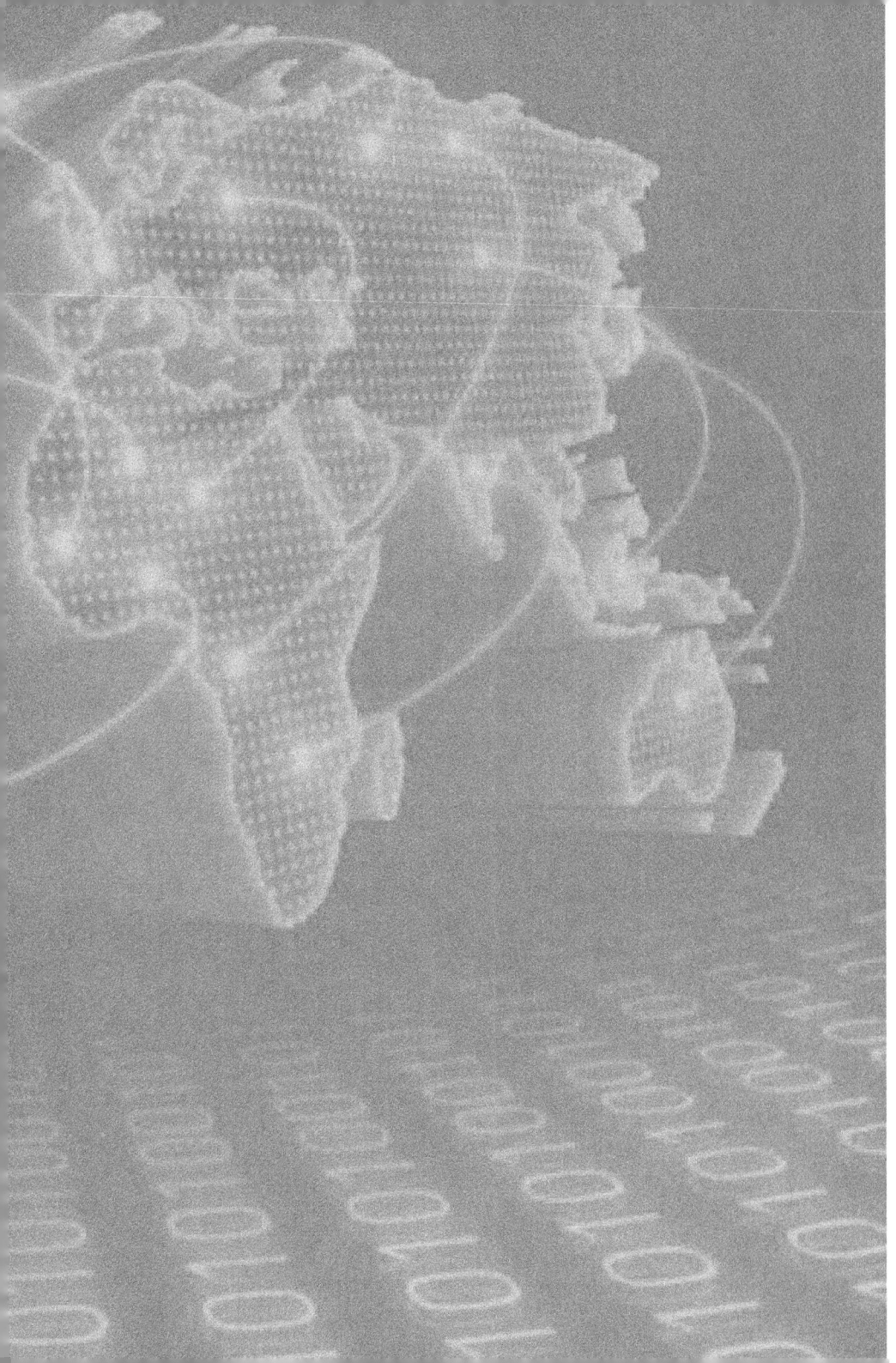

www.ingramcontent.com/pod-product-compliance
Lightning Source LLC
Chambersburg PA
CBHW071423200326
41520CB00014B/3548